The Wedding Vows
from
Conversations with God

Books by Neale Donald Walsch

The Wedding Vows
from
Conversations with God

Neale Donald Walsch
and
Nancy Fleming-Walsch

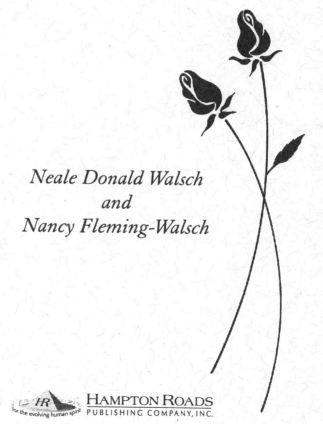

HAMPTON ROADS
PUBLISHING COMPANY, INC.

for the evolving human spirit

Cover design by Marjoram Productions
Cover and interior art by Anne Dunn

For information write:

Hampton Roads Publishing Company, Inc.
1125 Stoney Ridge Road
Charlottesville VA 22902

Or call: 804-296-2772
FAX: 804-296-5096
e-mail: hrpc@hrpub.com
Web site: www.hrpub.com

If you are unable to order this book from your local
bookseller, you may order directly from the publisher.
Quantity discounts for organizations are available.
Call 1-800-766-3009, toll-free.

Library of Congress Catalog Card Number: 99:95412

ISBN 1-57174-161-5

10 9 8 7 6 5 4 3 2 1

Printed on acid-free paper in Mexico

Table of Contents

*L*ove is that which is unlimited. There is no beginning and no end to it. No before and no after. Love always was, always is, and always will be.

CWG 3 p. 206

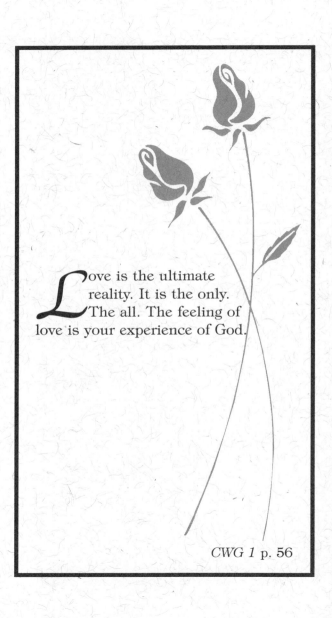

*L*ove is the ultimate reality. It is the only. The all. The feeling of love is your experience of God.

Introduction

If you are in love as you read this—if you have gone so far as to be planning your wedding and preparing for a life together with another—my heart sings for you! You are in a glorious place, experiencing a glorious feeling. This is the place of Divine Relationship, and what you are experiencing is All Encompassing Love. It is from this place that all creation springs. It is this song of love that all the universe sings. It is singing to you and through you now, and the heavens rejoice that its melody has found voice again on Earth.

You are embarking now on a wonderful journey, forming a partnership of the soul. This is the natural order of things, for in our world very little of your Self is best experienced or best expressed alone. It is only through your relationship with another person, place, or thing that you can experience yourself as anything at all while you are here in the Realm of the Relative. And the more magnificent your relationship with that other person, place, or thing, the more magnificent will be your experience of Self.

Relationship with another person in the partnership that we call marriage creates a perfect environment for magnificence expressed, for it is an outward manifestation of an inner truth about our actual state of being.

In truth, we are all married.

To everyone.

We are all one, and marriage can reflect this reality more vividly, more immediately, more continuously, more joyfully, and more impactfully than even you, as in love as you are right now, might imagine—if you use marriage as it was intended: not to get something from another, but to give something *to* another, and to share something *with* another, thus to know yourself *as* The Other.

This is the Divine Purpose of marriage, that the two shall truly become One.

Because marriage is the most intimate relationship you can have with another, it provides you with a chance to experience the most intimate relationship you have ever had with yourself. You can come to know yourself better as a result of marriage, and you can also become better than you know yourself to be, for marriage offers you with wonderful day-to-day, moment-to-moment opportunities to recreate yourself anew in the next grandest version of the greatest vision you ever held about Who You Are.

Used in these ways, your marriage will be a sacred experience—which is exactly what it was intended to be.

All things sacred are based in truth. You will want, therefore, everything about your marriage to be an expression of your own highest truth, including the words you say on your wedding day.

When Nancy and I decided to get married we looked around for the "right and perfect" wedding vows to exchange with each other. We wanted a ceremony that spoke the truth of our hearts, and that allowed us to make promises that we knew we could keep.

Nothing that we found from the more traditional sources, however, seemed to fit. We could have compromised, I suppose, and said what the ceremonies gave us to say, but we just didn't want to exchange words with each other on our wedding day that we knew we didn't mean literally. So we decided, as many couples do, to write our own vows. And we thought of them as wedding statements more than promises, out of our understanding that no one can really promise anything with a 100 percent guarantee, but that what we *could* do with integrity was make Statements of Intention. *Conversations with God* says that "life proceeds out of your intention for it," and so we knew that this was a very powerful place from which to come, not only on our wedding day, but every day of our lives.

Well, those Statements of Intention have produced some pretty amazing results. Nancy and I are having the most wonderful time of our lives. We are seeing that marriage can truly be experienced as an opportunity, not an obligation; as a place of growing excitement, not diminishing energy; as a chance for greater freedom, not less expression of the wonder of who we are.

One outcome that we did not expect, however, was that our wedding day statements would wind up being used by thousands of people around the world on their wedding day. It's happened because I got "talked into" placing the Statements of

Intention Nancy and I had written into the text of *Conversations with God, Book 3* as I was writing it. That was not something I had planned to do, but in the dialogue, as the discussion began to revolve around love relationships, I was invited to insert our wedding vows into the book as an example of how a spirit-centered, freedom-granting marriage ceremony might be created. I gave in to that impulse, never thinking that people all over the world would write, asking permission to use the ceremony and its statements for their own weddings.

Nancy and I knew, of course, that the statements were wonderful, because we could see the wonderful outcomes they had produced in our own lives. And I even had the idea as I placed them into *CWG* that they might one day be made available in a separate little book, for other couples to use—exactly as is, or in modified form—for their own marriage ceremonies. What I *didn't* think was that people would find the words that we wrote so right for them that they would begin using them immediately, copying them right out of the book, even before we could get this smaller book out!

Now as I look back on it, I can understand why we've received so many letters from couples telling us that "your marriage ceremony is just perfect for us!" I see that, like the *CWG* books themselves, these words were inspired by God—and were intended from the very beginning not for us alone, but to be shared with all the world.

So here they are, the wedding vows from *Conversations with God* (we've called them vows here in a bow to tradition, understanding that we are referring to the words of deep meaning that people exchange at the time of their marriage). Also included are some wonderful commentaries on life and love and romantic relationships from three people whom I love dearly: Jerry Jampolsky, Marianne Williamson, and my life partner, Nancy Fleming-Walsch.

This book comes to you from all of us, with love, and just the biggest hugs in our heart. We wish you every good idea God ever had about life, to be expressed and experienced by you and through you as you move into this breathtaking experience of your marriage and merger and soul partnership with your beloved.

Blesséd be.
Neale Donald Walsch

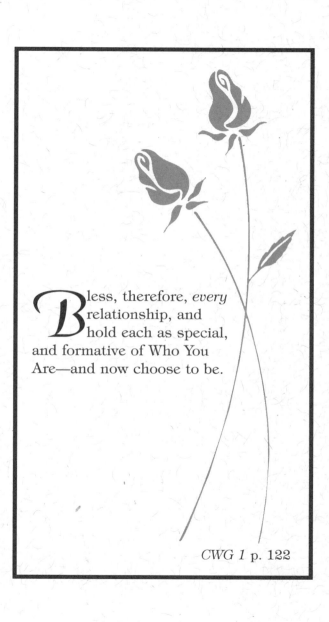

*B*less, therefore, *every* relationship, and hold each as special, and formative of Who You Are—and now choose to be.

CWG 1 p. 122

What love is, is
unlimited,
eternal, and free.
Therefore, that is
what *you* are. That is the
nature of Who You Are.

CWG 3 p. 221

To Lovers ... From Lovers:

Some Sacred Thoughts About Love

by Diane V. Cirincione, Ph.D.
and Gerald G. Jampolsky, M.D.

We had both been divorced seventeen years at the time of our marriage, and we had known each other nine years before making the decision to get married. Although we had a most close and loving relationship for those nine years, neither of us had been certain that marriage was the form of the relationship that we wanted with each other.

Then while on vacation in Hawaii, one evening while taking a walk on the beach at sunset time, we made a spiritual commitment to a relationship to each other. It was not just a "sort of" commitment, but a total commitment to put God first in our relationship and to devote our lives together in service as best we knew how, using God's Guidance. As the year went on, it was as if a door had become open and we felt guided to make a marriage commitment. We were married on the beach in Kihei, Hawaii, at 7 A.M. with Diane's parents and Wally and Christine Amos the only ones in attendance. We had a Lei ceremony for ourselves and for Wally and Christine and Diane's parents as well, who recommitted their relationship to love and to God.

At that time the power of our love seemed so beautiful, maximum, and AS FAR beyond this world as it could possibly be. Yet our love has grown even more deeply in magnitudes beyond our imagination. We feel so blessed to have our relationship be used by God to help others through our work with the more than 150 Center for Attitudinal Healing groups that are now located in more than 27 countries.

In our marriage we believe that how you start the day determines the day. This is so important to us that we wake up each day at 4:30 A.M. and we meditate and pray. We hold hands and say aloud a little prayer from

A Course in Miracles that puts the rudder in our ship before we even get out of bed. It goes like this:

> *I am not a body*
> *I am free*
> *For I am still as God Created me*
> *I want the Peace of God*
> *The Peace of God is my one goal*
> *The aim of all my living here*
> *My purpose, my function and my life*
> *While I abide when I am not at home*

Then we imagine our bodies turning into light and sending love to all those in our extended family and to those who are suffering from lack of love. We then go into silence and ask God for help in guiding us throughout the day. We frequently go on a silent meditation walk on the beach. (We live half the time in Hawaii and half the time in California.)

This relationship is different from any other relationship we have ever had because we both feel that we came in as whole people, rather than as a person with an empty space that the other person was supposed to fill.

Unconditional love, forgiveness, letting go of having any scripts for each other, and having God come first in our relationship has been essential to our marriage.

As we began to attempt to meet Nancy and Neale's request for some words for lovers who are committing themselves to marriage, what became very clear to us was that we do not know what is best for another couple.

We don't see ourselves as models for others. As a matter of fact, we feel that we had to create our own model.

We will attempt, however, to share with you what we feel has worked for us in a perhaps scattered, smorgasbord, non-sequential kind of way.

Some people believe that after the honeymoon is over romance will eventually fade away. We never chose to believe that. For us, romance and the excitement and adventure of living our lives together keeps increasing in magnitude each day of our lives.

Having the same interest in the other person as we do ourselves has been a mainstay of our marriage. Treating each other as equals, supporting each other's independence and guidance, letting go of trying to control the other person, not choosing to play the game of guilt and blame, committing ourselves to not be hurtful to each other, and taking responsibility for our own emotions have been part of the foundation of our relationship.

Taking responsibility for our own happiness and resisting the temptation to blame the other person when something goes wrong has been axiomatic. It is not that we are there all of the time, because we are not. But our strong intention to go in that direction is almost always there.

We absolutely love to be in nature. We love to do creative things together, like sculpting. We love to use our imagination to create romantic adventure together. For example, we spent one six-month period going one weekend a month to a bed and breakfast place that would be near a natural park that we wanted to explore.

Knowing when to turn off the telephones and to turn off the world has been important to us. Humor, laughing and giggling, and being silly has been a great elixir for getting over the hard spots.

Being able to ask each other for help, being able to totally listen and being totally present, and enjoying the silence with each other has been an important ingredient of our love, as well as not taking ourselves too seriously.

Letting go of assumptions and expectations, having acceptance, unconditional love, and not having a form for the other person to fit into has brought mountains and mountains of happiness to both of us. We both enjoy, every day, not taking the other person for granted, and telling the other person verbally and in many other ways how much we love and appreciate them.

Each of us still has the aura and excitement of being on our first date with each other. The romanticism and excitement of sexual intercourse is as if we are exploring and loving each other for the first time. Neither of us allow life to be boring. We find time to cuddle, hold hands, and touch each other a lot.

We give each other personal space. We resist the temptation to give each other unsolicited advice.

We are each other's best friend, and neither of us would ever dream of having a secret from the other. Trust and honesty are there all the time. We do our best to see the God-Self in each other. If there are conflicts, and they do occur, we commit to talking about it and resolving it before we go to bed. Rather than attacking each other and getting into the game of attack and defense, we ask each other for help. We look at each other without any shadows of the past.

We do our best to keep our relationship sacred and holy by wanting to give to each other, rather than attempting to get something from the other. Each moment of the day we love and let go and do our best to hang on to nothing.

Rather than worry about the future, we do our best to put the future into the hands of God. In striving to have a holy relationship, we believe that love and forgiveness are as important as breathing. It is a relationship where two lights come together, not only to light up each other, but to light up the whole world.

Diane wrote a poem early in our relationship that exemplifies this point and how she looks upon love.

If I love you above all others, it is because you have awakened in me capabilities for that much more love.

If I am to love all whom God has created as equal, then let me not love you less, to lower you to their level, but let me love them more and use you as a guiding light for my potential.

As I love God, I will seek to love you, and as my capacity to love grows, so will my awareness of love in others.

You are a luminescent catalyst for my love and for you I will be forever grateful.

To you lovers we would like to end our remarks by sharing with you some affirmations about commitment to marriage that we wrote for ourselves and that continue to serve us well:

May our blessed state of marriage, our holy relationship, be one in which God always comes first.

May our every thought, word, and action be accompanied by the thought of God from the time we awaken in the morning until the time we go to bed at night, and in our sleep as we rest.

May our love for each other and for God be a beacon of light that will nourish all others who may be suffering from lack of love.

May God's love always be in our hearts—reminding us that the purpose of our marriage is to have us teach each other—not patience, but infinite patience, tenderness, kindness, com-

passion, honesty, open-mindedness, tolerance, faith, and trust.

May we always be ready to forgive each other and to let go of all grievances and to love each other without judgments.

May our love continue to blossom and remain fresh and never become stale—by both of us having the willingness not to see any shadows in each other's past.

May we continue to remember that love is the answer to any possible problems that we might ever face, be they economical, emotional, or physical.

May we remember to teach only love to each other, not fear, and become teachers of love to each other, and to every one we might see.

May our will and God's Will always be one and the same.

May we continue to remember a loving God and trust in God and thereby know that God will never leave us abandoned or comfortless.

May love be the way we walk in gratitude every step of our lives as we continue to thank God for all of our blessings.

*T*here is only one sacred
promise—and that is to
tell and live your truth.

CWG 3 p. 210

The Truest Heart

by Marianne Williamson

Intimate love is full of challenges, presenting as it so often does our greatest opportunities for both joy and sorrow. Who among us can honestly say we have never been wounded by the arrows of love?

According to the tenets of ageless spiritual wisdom, all pain derives from spiritual ignorance. What, then, is our ignorance in the face of romantic love? What is it we're not seeing, or thinking, that makes us so prone to romantic pain?

We are drawn toward fire, when drawn to the heart of another. We are drawn to the experience of God there, because God *is* the experience of our oneness. We are healed in that place, yet healing is not always easy.

Yes, there is initial excitement, to be sure, when we find ourselves face to face with a beloved. But then the moment surely comes, when we are not comforted by love so much as our egos are burned by it. For love is a trial of initiation, where all that is not our truest selves—the most authentic expression of our highest potential—is cast into the fires of divine, transformative alchemy.

Once I really, truly see you, I will see that you are not perfect. You are a human being, just like me, and your fears run deep, exactly like mine. You have not transcended all of your fears any more than I have transcended all of mine. And now, in this moment, both our weaknesses and strengths in tow, we walk this Earth together. Will we connect through our weaknesses, or connect through our strengths? Will we abandon each other, or forgive each other? Will we further hurt each other by triggering our wounds, or heal each other by our compassion for them? Those are the questions which are posed by love.

Romance demands a hero's heart, yet it is often met with a cowardly narcissism. Romantic love is a quest; it is not just a gift. It is a noble pursuit and a challenging path.

To approach it lightly is to not approach it at all.

Love is in fact a mystical pursuit, for it is a search for the light at the center of things. It is a ride to heaven, best taken with a mystical passenger to guide the journey. The key to success in romantic love is the power of a mystical Third.

We can invoke an inner room for love, a sanctuary built by our commitment to forgive, where both of us are comforted and shielded and healed. There is activated there a vortex of power, in which our deliverance to the highest dimensions of love is both guided and protected by angels.

Angels are the thoughts of God.

You are not my enemy, you are my brother.
That thought is an angel.

I choose not to bind you, but to free you.
That thought is an angel.

May I be a source of love in all things.
That thought is an angel.

May our love deliver both of us
to who we most truly are, that we
might better serve the world.
That thought is an angel.

Angels surround us on all our paths. Hearing them, and heeding them, is the holy grail of love.

What we yearn for most is to go home together—to really go home. And for that, we need more than each other's arms: we need each other's forgiveness and compassion and stalwart loyalty. Finding that, we find a smiling God.

From our ecstatic joining, we create new life. As bodies join to conceive a child, minds and spirits join to recreate the lives we are already living With the material womb we give birth to babies; with the spiritual womb, made active by the union of masculine and feminine within, we give birth to the energies of our own transformation. Boys become men, when they learn to love. And girls become women, when we learn to love. That passage, from who we used to be to who we are capable of becoming, is the greatest hope for the healing of the human race. It is a miracle of birth, no less than is the birth of a physical child. It is no less joyous, it is no less painful, it is no less miraculous, and it is no less holy. It is not always easy and it is not always fun. But it is always, always, always worth it. There is a joy in our finally making it, that makes the world as we know it fade away, and heaven reappear at last.

The truest heart is a hopeful heart. We are always on our way, when we are on our way together.

W e are *all* married.
We are married to
each other—now,
and forevermore.

CWG 3 p. 243

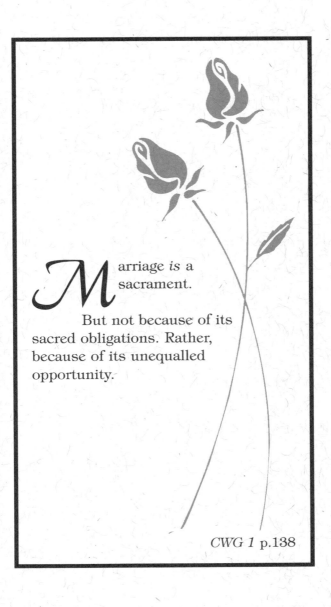

$\mathcal{M}$arriage *is* a sacrament.

But not because of its sacred obligations. Rather, because of its unequalled opportunity.

CWG 1 p.138

*T*hrough the corridors of all human experience has this Truth been echoed: *love is the answer.*

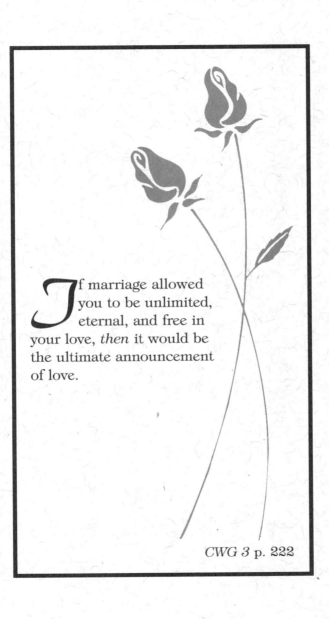

If marriage allowed you to be unlimited, eternal, and free in your love, *then* it would be the ultimate announcement of love.

CWG 3 p. 222

The Wedding Vows

Minister:

       _____ and _____ have not come here on this day to make a solemn promise or to exchange a sacred vow. They have already done that, long ago in their hearts.

       _____ and _____ have come here to make public their commitment; to give noticement to their promise; to say again their vow—out loud and in your presence, out of their desire that we will all come to feel a very real and intimate part of their decision, and thus make it even more powerful.

They've also come here in the further hope that their ritual of bonding will help bring us all closer together. If you are here with a spouse or a partner, let this ceremony be a reminder—a rededication of your own loving bond.

We'll begin by asking the question: Why get married? _____ and _____ have answered this question for themselves, and they've told me their answer. Now I want to ask them one more time, so they can be sure of their answer, certain of their understanding, and firm in their commitment to the truth they share.

(Minister gets two red roses from table . . .)

This is the Ceremony of Roses, in which _____ and _____ share their understandings, and commemorate that sharing.

Now _____ and _____, you have told me it is your firm understanding that you are not entering into this marriage for reasons of security . . .

. . . that the only real security is not in owning or possessing, nor in being owned or possessed . . .

. . . not in demanding or expecting, and not even in hoping, that what you think you need in life will be supplied by the other . . .

. . . but rather, in knowing that everything you need in life . . . all the love, all the wisdom, all the insight, all the power, all the knowledge, all the understanding, all the nurturing, all the compassion, and all the strength . . . resides within you . . .

. . . and that you are not each marrying the other in hopes of getting these things, but in hopes of giving these gifts, that the other might have them in even greater abundance.

Is that your firm understanding now?

(They say, "It is.")

And _____ and _____, you have told me it is your firm understanding you are not entering into this marriage as a means of in any way limiting, controlling, hindering, or restricting each other from any true expression and honest celebration of that which is the highest and best within you—including your love of God, your love of life, your love of people, your love of creativity, your love of work, or any aspect of your being which genuinely represents you, and brings you joy. Is that still your firm understanding now?

(They say, "It is.")

Finally, _____ and _____, you have said to me that you do not see marriage as producing obligations, but rather as providing opportunities . . .

. . . opportunities for growth, for full Self-expression, for lifting your lives to their highest potential, for healing every false thought or small idea you ever had about yourself, and for ultimate reunion with God through the communion of your two souls . . .

. . . that this is truly a Holy communion . . . a journey through life with one you love as an equal partner, sharing equally both the authority and the responsibilities inherent in any partnership, bearing equally what burdens there be, basking equally in the glories.

Is that the vision you wish to enter into now?

(They say "It is.")

I now give you these red roses, symbolizing your individual understandings of these Earthly things; that you both know and agree how life will be with you in bodily form, and within the physical structure called marriage. Give these roses now to each other as a symbol of your sharing of these agreements and understandings with love.

Now, please each of you take this white rose. It is a symbol of your larger understandings, of your spiritual nature and your spiritual truth. It stands for the purity of your Real and Highest Self, and of the purity of God's love, which shines upon you now, and always.

(She gives the groom a rose which has his ring pre-placed on the stem, and the bride the rose with her ring on it.)

What symbols do you bring as a reminder of the promises given and received today?

(They each remove the rings from the stems, giving them to the minister, who holds them in her hand as she says . . .)

A circle is the symbol of the Sun, and the Earth, and the Universe. It is a symbol of holiness, and of perfection and peace. It is also the symbol of the eternality of spiritual truth, love, and life . . . that which has no beginning and no end. And in this moment, _____ and _____ choose for it to also be a symbol of unity, but not of possession; of joining, but not of restricting; of encirclement; but not of entrapment. For love cannot be possessed, nor can it be restricted. And the soul can never be entrapped.

Now _____ and _____, please take these rings you wish to give, one to the other.

(They take each other's rings)

_____, please repeat after me.

I, _____ . . . ask you, _____ . . . to be my partner, my lover, my friend, and my wife . . . I announce and declare my intention to give you my deepest friendship and love . . . not only when your moments are high . . . but when they are low . . . not only when you remember clearly Who You Are . . . but when you forget . . . not only when you are acting with love . . . but when you are not . . . I further announce before God and those here present . . . that I will seek always to see the Light of Divinity within you . . . and seek always to share the Light of Divinity within me . . . even, and especially in whatever moments of darkness may come.

It is my intention to be with you forever . . . in a Holy Partnership of the soul . . . that we may do together God's work . . . sharing all that is good within us . . . with all those whose lives we touch.

(The minister turns to the bride.)

_____, do you choose to grant _____'s request that you be his wife?

(She answers, "I do.")

Now _____, please repeat after me. I, _____ . . . ask you, _____ . . . to be my partner, my lover, my friend, and my husband . . . I announce and declare my intention to give you my deepest friendship and love . . . not only when your moments are high . . . but when they are low . . . not only when you remember clearly Who You Are . . . but when you forget . . . not only when you are acting with love . . . but when you are not . . . I further announce before God and those here present . . . that I will seek always to see the Light of Divinity within you . . . and seek always to share the Light of Divinity within me . . . even, and especially in whatever moments of darkness may come.

It is my intention to be with you forever . . . in a Holy Partnership of the soul . . . that we may do together God's work . . . sharing all that is good within us . . . with all those whose lives we touch.

(The minister turns to the groom.)

_____, do you choose to grant _____'s request that you be her husband?

(He answers, "I do.")

Please then, both of you, take hold of the rings you would give each other, and repeat after me: With this ring . . . I thee wed . . . I take now your ring . . . (they exchange rings) . . . and give it place upon my hand . . . (they place the rings on their hands) . . . that all may see and know of my love for you.

We recognize with full awareness that only a couple can administer the sacrament of marriage to each other, and only a couple can sanctify it. Neither a church, nor any power vested in me by the state, can grant me the authority to declare what only two hearts can declare, and what only two souls can make real.

And so now, inasmuch as you, _____, and you, _____, have announced the truths that are already written in your hearts, and have witnessed the same in the presence of these, your friends, and the One Living Spirit—we observe joyfully that you have declared yourself to be . . . husband and wife.

Let us now join in prayer.

Spirit of Love and life: out of this whole world, two souls have found each other. Their destinies shall now be woven into one design, and their perils and their joys shall not be known apart.

_____ and _____, may your home be a place of happiness for all who enter it; a place where the old and the young are renewed in each other's company, a place for growing and a place for sharing, a place for music and a place for laughter, a place for prayer and a place for love.

May those who are nearest to you be constantly enriched by the beauty and the bounty of your love for one another, may your work be a joy of your life that serves the world, and may your days be good, and long upon the Earth.

Amen, and amen.

*R*elationships are
sacred because they
provide life's grandest
opportunity—indeed, its only
opportunity—to create and
produce the *experience* of your
highest conceptualization of
Self.

CWG 1 p. 124

And They Lived
Happily Ever After

by Nancy Fleming-Walsch

How many times have we heard those words at the end of wonderful love stories or fairy tales? These love stories so often end with the two lovers finally getting together, bonding permanently, and living in bliss from that moment onward. But marriage is the beginning, not the end, of a true love story. And that is what I want to tell you here. I want to send you this message as you embark on your own journey into love. This is the *beginning*, this step that you are about to take, not the end-all.

It is unfortunate that for many people the love that originally brought them together starts dissipating, rather than really just beginning to blossom, after the wedding. Yet there is another way, and I have experienced that with my life partner, Neale, and so I know that it works. I can say that Neale and I are actually *more* in love with each other now than the day we were married—and that is saying a lot, because, of course, we were very much in love on that day.

There are many things that have contributed to the joy that Neale and I experience together, and, as I have pondered what I might say in this wonderful little booklet of wedding vows, I have been looking at what would be helpful to others. First, let me share that this is not my first marriage. So I was beginning to think that the real love, the kind that lasts and lasts and grows bigger and better, really *was* "just a fairy tale." All that I experienced, and heard about from my friends, was a love that deteriorated over time. So now, after five years of marriage with Neale. I am looking back and asking, "What's different? What keeps our love growing?"

One thing I know is that each of us is unique, and each relationship is unique, and so there is no one set of perfect answers. It is not even as if my relationship with Neale is perfect, or is guaranteed to bring us life-long happiness. In fact, that brings me to my first point—and, perhaps, my most important one: The future is never guaranteed. Marriage vows are statements of *intention*, not guarantees. Anyone who thinks that marriage is a guarantee of eternal happiness is going to be disappointed. Yet everyone who understands that it is our *intention* which forms our reality will see that happiness *can* grow, and love *can* expand, as each year passes.

Intentions, however, are announced not only on your wedding day, but every day of your life. In my case with Neale, this is specifically true. Each day, Neale and I tell each other our choices and intentions. We take a spontaneous moment to look into each other's eyes and hand each other our wedding rings and take turns placing the rings back on each other's hand. And we say, "I choose you again this day." No big deal is made of it, and we don't panic if a day is missed, but we are amazed at how such a small gesture has produced wonderful and amazing results, increasing our intimacy and reaffirming our original choice to love each other always, through everything.

After hearing that Neale and I do this,

one person asked me, "What happens if, on a certain day, you don't feel very loving? Maybe there's a recent disagreement that hasn't been solved, or something else has come up, and you just don't feel like saying 'I choose you again.' Then what?"

I stopped and thought about this. It was a good question. I told her that Neale and I rarely have disagreements that would stop us from feeling loving toward each other; but if we do, that's when I find out what my true intentions for our marriage are, and what is important to me. I know that each day is a new day, with new challenges, but each day I re-look at what my priorities are, and at that wonderful question posed in *Conversations with God*, "What would love do now?" It is at this point that I know that choosing Neale again is what I want—*not because of a past promise*, but because, right here, right now, that is my decision. There are other factors in my relationship which have made this choice each day an easy one. Let me share some more of them with you.

Neale and I drop as many of our expectations as possible. It is difficult to not have expectations. After all, didn't that fairy tale say "happily ever after?" Yet what works for me is turning my expectations of Neale into preferences. I learned this after, in the early going, I would find my happiness shattered if some things didn't go a certain way with us. I knew it was my expectations that created that sadness, not the actual turn of events. Yet I discovered that if I experienced my desired outcomes as *preferences* rather than *expectations*, my happiness wasn't nearly so affected if they didn't occur.

As our marriage vows say, Neale is not here to please me. When I learned that I was responsible for my own happiness, then the "happily ever after" really started occurring.

Another factor in our happiness is the level of communication that has developed between Neale and me. This has grown, I am sure, from our intention to not make assumptions, and to share any expectations or preferences that come up. We listen to each other. We actually *like* listening to each other. We make *time* to do this, every day. I think that is very important. It doesn't take a huge chunk out of our schedule. We're not talking about hours and hours here. A few minutes upon awaking, a moment before turning in, a quiet talk in the car as we're driving, whenever and wherever it is, Neale and I find a time each day—some days, several times—to share with each other. Truth is, we never *miss* a chance to share what's in our hearts and on our minds. That's what is wonderful about our relationship, and that's what I hope you will do in yours. Marriage is no place for tight lips. Love is no place for holding back.

This frequent and open communication in our relationship has been one of our greatest blessings. We share our thoughts, feelings, desires, and even our sad moments. Neale has taught me how to make it safe, by listening and hearing. And, in turn, I try to give him the same gift.

One thing that Neale does naturally, and that I have had to learn to do, is to pay a sincere compliment whenever possible. I have never known a man who has had more nice things to say in any twenty-four hour period. And he doesn't make them up. If he can't say them honestly, he doesn't say them. I have picked up on this habit, and it is, I can tell you, an incredible way to stay in a positive frame of mind, not just about each other, but about life itself.

If you look for positive things, you will find them, but here is what is magical: The more you see and share positive things about others, the more others begin feeling positive about themselves—and suddenly, *there are a lot more positive things showing up*! This can't be idle flattery, and, again, as in our restatement of choice, this is no big deal with Neale and me. There are no rules, no "should's." It's just about sharing out loud when you see something that you admire. *Even if you've shared it a million times before.* (You can never hear, "I love the way your hair falls over your forehead," enough. You can never be told, "That was so considerate. That is just like you," enough.)

Now this may seem so easy to do. Yet when the days become hectic and frustrations build, it may not be as easy as it sounds. Still, it is at just those times that it is even more cherished.

Here's another important factor in what makes my present relationship different from all the others, and this factor is what these marriage vows are all about: letting others be "who they are."

Accept and love others and allow them freedom of expression. This is one of the greatest gifts you can give your partner, and an expression of the most wonderful kind of love we could ever imagine—the love of God. In my relationship with Neale, each person is allowed to live authentically. If limits are placed on another by you, you will never have the full knowing of whether that other is choosing what you want out of their desire, or yours.

And that leads me to another observation. Change within relationships is inevitable.

Change is a gift. The process of evolution and growth will produce change in you and your partner. True love allows for the possibility of true change, it never inhibits it.

What we are talking about here is freedom. The freedom in these marriage vows provides the opportunity to be the grandest version of the greatest vision you ever held about yourselves—including changing and reaching new heights. These vows have given Neale and me the ability to grow and be our authentic selves.

At first I thought such freedom was impossible to allow. I got into my fear of loss. But with stepping to the edge, testing it out, talking, and sharing, I learned that I could fly, rather than fall. The love and commitment between us has grown just as we have been able to grow as individuals. So I have concluded: *When individuals cannot grow, love cannot grow*.

See marriage as producing opportunities, not obligations, just as the vows say. Opportunities for growth, rather than obligations that stunt growth, or make it actually impossible.

Even though Neale and I have grown and changed in our relationship, our desire and goal of "doing God's work, and sharing all that is good within us with all those whose lives we touch," hasn't changed. With this goal leading and guiding our marriage, we have a foundation on which to build our lives. We are moving in the same direction. And that is the final factor I think of that makes my relationship with Neale work so much better: a shared agenda.

By this I don't mean that we can't or don't have different interests, but that our overall life agenda is held in common. Our largest goals are the same.

Marriage can be a wonderful way to express Who You Really Are. I hope that each day you will reaffirm who you choose to be in relationship to this thing called "marriage." Enjoy what life brings you on your road of matrimony, and *create* your "happily ever after."

I wish for all of you who are taking this next step in a relationship—this most wonderful, glorious, exciting, dynamic, hugely loving step—all the joy and happiness that lives now in your heart, forever and ever.

$\mathcal{F}$or I tell you this: at the critical juncture in all human relationships, there is only one question:

What would Love do now?

CWG 1 p. 138

Afterword and Closing Prayer

As you prepare now for your own wedding, for the marriage of souls that will define so much of how your life is and what it is about from this time forward, I hope that you and your partner will undertake a genuine and serious study of all of the material relating to relationships in the *With God* series of books.

The *Conversations with God* trilogy, and its sequels, *Friendship with God* and *Communion with God*, offer wonderful—I want to say, extraordinary—insights into human love, romantic relationships, and every important human interaction, and provide you with the tools with which to elevate them to newer and higher levels. Check the index in the back of each of those books for specific references to Relationship, Sexuality, and Love.

Now I want you to know that I am aware that some of what you've read here in the commentaries from Jerry, Marianne, and Nancy duplicates itself. These commentaries were written at different times, in different places, by different people, and yet there are many common threads. When I first received these writings, I thought of editing some of the redundancy out. Then I realized that more would be served by leaving it in. I think that the fact that so many principles of sound relationships have been arrived at independently and repeated, each in their own way, by different people, is a statement in itself.

I wish you well now as you embark on your journey, inviting you to make of your new life together a sparkling and enduring testimony to the wonder of love and the truth of Who You Really Are.

I asked Marianne, who is the minister at the Church of Today in Warren, Michigan, if she could put a conclusion on this little book in the form of a prayer. Thank you, Marianne, for gifting us with this, and I invite each of you to read this now, as you begin focusing on your upcoming marriage in your daily *conversations with God*. . . .

Neale Donald Walsch

Dear God,

As we embark upon this miraculous journey,
may our hearts be lifted up in joy.
May my beloved see in me,
and I see in my beloved,
the innocence in which You created us.
Remove from us the barriers to love.
Deliver us to the brightest light,
where forgiveness is our constant guide
and peace our constant friend.
Bless our relationship,
bless our marriage,
and through us
bless the world.

Amen

_____

and

_____

have joined together in love
to share a lifetime.

On this day

_____

at

_____

in

_____

Hampton Roads Publishing Company

. . . for the evolving human spirit

Hampton Roads Publishing Company
publishes books on a variety of subjects including
metaphysics, health, complementary medicine,
visionary fiction, and other related topics.

For a copy of our latest catalog,
call toll-free, 800-766-8009,
or send your name and address to:

Hampton Roads Publishing Company, Inc.
1125 Stoney Ridge Road
Charlottesville, VA 22902

e-mail: hrpc@hrpub.com
www.hrpub.com